GRAPHIC LIBRARY

GRAPHIC BIOGRAPHIES

JIM THORPE
GREATEST ATHLETE IN THE WORLD

by Jennifer Fandel
illustrated by Rod Whigham

Consultant:
Mark Dyreson
Associate Professor of Kinesiology and History
Penn State University

Capstone
press

Mankato, Minnesota

Graphic Library is published by Capstone Press,
1710 Roe Crest Drive, North Mankato, Minnesota 56003.
www.capstonepub.com

Books published by Capstone Press are manufactured with paper
containing at least 10 percent post-consumer waste.

Library of Congress Cataloging-in-Publication Data
Fandel, Jennifer.
    Jim Thorpe: greatest athlete in the world / by Jennifer Fandel; illustrated by
Rod Whigham.
    p. cm.—(Graphic biographies) (Graphic library)
    Includes bibliographical references and index.
    ISBN-13: 978-1-4296-0152-8 (hardcover)   ISBN-10: 1-4296-0152-3 (hardcover)
    ISBN-13: 978-1-4296-1773-4 (softcover pbk.)   ISBN-10: 1-4296-1773-X (softcover pbk.)
    1. Thorpe, Jim, 1887–1953. 2. Athletes—Biography—Juvenile literature. I. Whigham, Rod,
1954– II. Title. III. Series.
GV697.T5F36 2008
796.092—dc22   2007000286
[B]

Summary: In graphic novel format, tells the life story of Jim Thorpe, star of the 1912 Olympic
Games and member of the Pro Football Hall of Fame.

Designers
Thomas Emery and Kyle Grenz

Colorist
Kim Brown

Editor
Tom Adamson

Editor's note: Direct quotations from primary sources are indicated by a yellow background.

Direct quotations appear on the following pages:
Pages 6, 13, 15, 16, 23, 24, from *All American: The Rise and Fall of Jim Thorpe*, by Bill
    Crawford (Hoboken, N.J.: John Wiley & Sons, 2005).

Printed in the United States of America in Stevens Point, Wisconsin.

Meet the Author

JUWANDA G. FORD says, "When I was a little girl, I loved visiting my neighborhood barbershop. I always left feeling as if I had just been to a good friend's house. However, I didn't consider writing about a barbershop until I met my husband, Alton Williams. He had just started working at the real All Star Barbershop in Brooklyn, New York, when I went in for a haircut. Since then, I often spend time in The Shop. I've noticed that when young boys come in, they shake hands, watch a game, and even order lunch along with everyone else. They leave feeling confident and happy!"

Juwanda G. Ford was born and raised in New Orleans, Louisiana, and attended college in Texas and Oxford, England. She and her husband Alton make their home in Brooklyn, New York. She has worked for several children's book publishers but is now a full-time freelance writer. *Sunday Best* is another JUST FOR YOU! Book she has written.

Meet the Artist

JIM HOSTON says, "I really enjoyed working on this book because a barbershop is such a cool place. You can go there to find out the latest news and catch up with friends—and everyone knows your name! After reading Juwanda's story, I just had to meet her and see the real thing for myself. I visited The All Star Barbershop and took photos of Alton and the rest of the crew. I used these photos as reference when I painted the scenes for this book."

Jim Hoston's beautiful portraits and other paintings have been exhibited in galleries in several cities. Jim and his wife live in Brooklyn, New York, and he maintains a studio there. He also commutes to Boston, Massachusetts, where he works as a professor in the illustration department of The Art Institute of Boston. *Shop Talk* is the fourth children's book he has illustrated.

YOUR Favorite Place

Solomon says that the barbershop is his favorite place.
Why do you think he likes it so much?

Think about YOUR neighborhood. What's your favorite place to
visit? Why do you like it? What do you do there? Draw a picture
of that place. Show what makes the place special to YOU!

▲▲▲▲TOGETHER TIME ▲▲▲▲

*Make some time to share ideas about the story with your young reader!
Here are some activities you can try. There are no right or wrong
answers!*

Think About It: Ask your child, "Why don't the men in the barbershop speak to Mrs. Williams the same way they speak to each other?
How does this show respect?" Play a thinking game: How many
different ways can the two of you think of to say hello? Why do you
use different greetings for different people?

Read It Again: The author and illustrator give clues to help readers
figure out how Solomon feels. What clues tell you when he is feeling
happy? How about when he's feeling proud? Read the story aloud
together, and read with feeling! Your child can read Solomon's words,
while you read what the other characters have to say.

Talk About It: Read about the author and artist on page 32. Many
details in the story and pictures are based on real people and places.
Look carefully at the author's photo. Can your child find a character
in the story who looks like her? Talk about why the artist might have
put her in his pictures. What other details might come from real life?